The Countries

Iraq

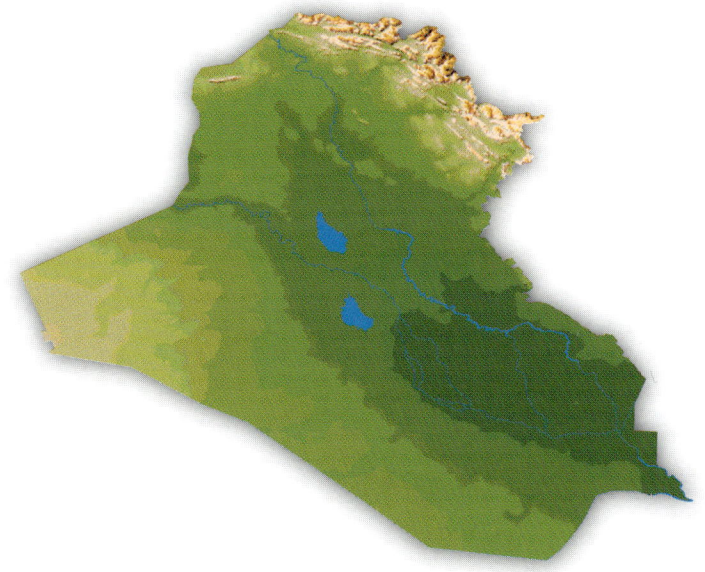

Tamara L. Britton
ABDO Publishing Company

visit us at
www.abdopub.com

Published by ABDO Publishing Company, 4940 Viking Drive, Suite 622, Edina, Minnesota 55435. Copyright © 2000 Abdo Consulting Group, Inc., Pentagon Tower, P.O. Box 36036, Minneapolis, Minnesota 55435 USA. International copyrights reserved in all countries. No part of this book may be reproduced in any form without written permission from the publisher.

Printed in the United States.

Interior Photos: AP Wideworld Photos, Corbis
Editors: Bob Italia and Kate A. Furlong
Art Direction & Maps: Pat Laurel

Library of Congress Cataloging-in-Publication Data

Britton, Tamara L., 1963-
   Iraq / Tamara L. Britton.
      p. cm. -- (The Countries)
   Includes index.
   Summary: Brief text explores the history, geography, government, cities, recreation, and people of the oil-rich Middle Eastern country.
   ISBN 1-57765-392-0
   1. Iraq--Juvenile literature. [1. Iraq.] I. Title. II. Series.

DS70.62 .B75 2000
956.7--dc21

                                                                                                            00-026643

Contents

Ahalan! 4
Fast Facts 6
Timeline 7
An Ancient Civilization 8
The Land Between Two Rivers 14
Iraq's Plants & Animals 18
Iraq's Government 20
Making Money 22
Iraq's Beautiful Cities 24
Iraq on the Go 28
Citizens of Iraq 30
Happy Holidays 34
Relaxing in Iraq 36
Glossary 38
Web Sites 39
Index 40

Ahalan!

Hello! Welcome to Iraq. Iraq has made important **contributions** to the world. Its ancient societies gave the world farming, writing, and wheeled carts. And its oil reserves are some of the world's largest.

Iraq is in the Middle East between the Tigris and Euphrates Rivers. It has deserts, plains, mountains, and rolling hills. These different kinds of land make homes for many different plants and animals.

Iraq has a strong **economy**. Its land produces much of the world's oil. Iraqi farmers grow dates, wheat, rice, and vegetables.

There are large, modern cities in Iraq. Baghdad is Iraq's capital. It was founded in A.D. 762. Iraq's cities are centers of culture. The largest cities have museums, theaters, and ancient ruins.

Iraq's people are mostly Arab **Muslims**. But some of the people are Kurds. The Kurds want to have their own country. They fight with Iraq over land. Even with their differences, Iraqis have happy homes. They go to movies and museums, play soccer, and write poetry.

Iraq's government is a republic. It wants all Iraqis to share in their nation's wealth. But the government is **aggressive** against other nations. It has attacked other countries and started wars.

This aggression has resulted in **sanctions** against Iraq. These sanctions make it hard for Iraqis to live well. They cannot sell their oil or buy goods from other countries.

Even with the sanctions, Iraqis are strong. That is why Iraq has lasted thousands of years and **contributed** much to the world.

An Iraqi girl in a chador, the head covering worn by female Muslims.

Iraq

Fast Facts

OFFICIAL NAME: Republic of Iraq

CAPITAL: Baghdad

LAND
- Area: 168,730 square miles (437,072 sq. km)
- Mountain Ranges: Zagros
- Highest point: Mount Halgurd 12,230 feet (3,728 m)
- Lowest point: Persian Gulf sea level
- Major Rivers: Tigris, Euphrates, and Shatt al-Arab
- Lakes: Al-Hammar, As-Saniyah, and Wadi Ath-Tharthar
- Deserts: Wadiyah, Al-Hijarah

PEOPLE
- Population: 22,427,150 (July 1999)
- Major Cities: Baghdad, Basra, Mosul
- Language: Arabic (official), Kurdish (official in Kurdistan)
- Religion: Islam (official)

GOVERNMENT
- Form: Republic
- Head: President
- Legislature: National Assembly
- Flag: Red, white, and black horizontal stripes. In the white stripe there are three stars. Between the stars are the words "God is Great."
- National Anthem: "Al-Salaam al-Jumhuri" ("Salute of the Republic")
- Nationhood: October 3, 1932

ECONOMY
- Agricultural Products: dates, barley, wheat, rice, vegetables, corn, millet, sugarcane, sugar beets, oil seeds, fruit, fodder, tobacco, and cotton
- Mining Products: oil, natural gas, coal, iron, lead, copper
- Manufactured Products: military hardware, tractors, electrical goods, telephone cable, tires, food products
- Money: 1,000 fils = 20 dirhams = 1 dinar

Iraq's Flag

A marketplace in Iraq

Timeline

4000 B.C.	Sumerians live in Mesopotamia (present-day Iraq)
1792 B.C.	King Hammurabi rules Mesopotamia
539 B.C.	Cyrus the Great conquers Mesopotamia
330 B.C.	Alexander the Great conquers Mesopotamia
A.D. 637	Abbasids conquer Mesopotamia
762	Capital moves to Baghdad
1258	Mongols conquer Baghdad
1530s	Turks conquer Mesopotamia
1918	British control area after World War I
1921	Faisal I elected king
1932	Iraq becomes an independent nation
1933	King Faisal I dies
1939	King Ghazi dies, his brother al-Ilah rules
1953	Faisal II becomes king
1958	Revolution, King Faisal II killed, Iraq declared a republic
1968	Saddam Hussein leads coups against premier and president
1979	Al-Bakr resigns, Hussein now president and premier
1980	Iraq declares war on Iran
1990	Iraq invades Kuwait, United Nations impose economic sanctions against Iraq

An Ancient Civilization

In ancient times, present-day Iraq was called Mesopotamia. This means "land between two rivers." Sumerians, Babylonians, Arabs, and Turks prospered in Mesopotamia. They made important **contributions** to the world. For this reason, Iraq is known as the cradle of civilization.

The Sumerians had an advanced society. In about 4000 B.C., they became the first farmers. They also invented a calendar and a writing system called cuneiform. And they built the first two-wheeled cart. The Sumerians were very successful. So, many other peoples tried to attack their land. Soon, the Sumerian civilization broke up.

In 1792 B.C., King Hammurabi reunited the people of Mesopotamia into one kingdom. He called it Babylon. And he created the Code of Hammurabi. This was one of the first sets of organized laws.

An ancient Sumerian used this cuneiform tablet to keep track of his sheep and goats.

The Code of Hammurabi carved in stone

After King Hammurabi died in 1750 B.C., the Assyrians conquered Babylon and ruled Mesopotamia. Soon, King Nebuchadnezzar II rebuilt Babylon. He built the hanging gardens of Babylon. They were one of the seven wonders of the ancient world.

After King Nebuchadnezzar died, Mesopotamia was conquered many times. Cyrus the Great ruled Mesopotamia in 539 B.C. Alexander the Great conquered it in 330 B.C.

In the second century A.D., Mesopotamia became part of the Persian Empire. In A.D. 637, Arab **Muslims**, called Abbasids, conquered the land. In A.D. 762, the Abbasids moved the capital from Babylon to Baghdad. They ruled for many years until A.D. 1258, when Mongols conquered Baghdad.

After years of disorder, Turks took control of Mesopotamia. They ruled it from the 1530s until 1918. After World War I, the British controlled Baghdad. In 1921, Iraq elected a king and became a **constitutional monarchy**. On October 3, 1932, Iraq finally became an independent country. Emir Faisal was its first king.

Alexander the Great

King Faisal I

King Faisal I died in 1933. His son Ghazi became king. King Ghazi formed an **alliance** with other Arab nations. But in 1939, King Ghazi died in a car crash. His son Faisal was only four years old. So, King Ghazi's brother Abd al-Ilah governed Iraq until Faisal was old enough to be king.

During World War II, the British occupied Iraq again. Iraq became an important supply post for the **Allies**. In 1945, Iraq was a founding member of the Arab League, and also joined the **United Nations (UN)**.

In 1948, Iraq was part of an Arab force that invaded Israel. The Arabs were unhappy that the new country of Israel was part of the sacred land of **Palestine**. In 1949, agreements were made between the Arabs and the Israelis. But the Arabs were still upset with Israel.

King Ghazi

In May 1953, King Ghazi's son Faisal was old enough to become king. King Faisal II made treaties with Western countries. This angered Arab citizens. They wanted to be connected with other Arab countries, not the West. So, on July 14, 1958, General Karim Kassem led a military **coup**. They killed King Faisal II. And the country became a republic.

An Ancient Civilization

After the **coup**, Iraq's government was in disorder. On July 17, 1968, the army overthrew the government and came into power. Many important army officers were members of the Ba'th Party. The Ba'th Party believed in strong Arab nations and **socialism** based on **Islamic** beliefs. The Ba'th-controlled government made Abd ar-Razzaq al-Nayif the new **premier**.

The government then created the Revolutionary Command Council (RCC). The RCC became Iraq's highest authority. It elected Ahmad Hassan al-Bakr as president of the republic. On July 30, 1968, Saddam Hussein, a leader in the Ba'th Party, staged a coup against al-Nayif. Now, al-Bakr was premier as well as president.

The new government wanted all Iraqis to share in their country's success. The government grew more crops. It took control of the oil **industry**. And it gave land to peasants, so they didn't have to pay rent to landowners.

King Faisal II (left) and Abd al-Ilah on Faisal's eighteenth birthday

Iraq

Ahmad Hassan al-Bakr

During the 1970s, Iraq went to war with the Kurds. The Kurds wanted their own country. They were getting supplies and money from Iran. This angered Iraq. Iran and Iraq were also fighting over the border between the two countries. The war with the Kurds ended when Iran stopped supporting them. The Kurds briefly stopped their **rebellion**.

On July 16, 1979, al-Bakr stepped down. Saddam Hussein became president. On June 20, 1980, Iraq held general elections to choose its lawmakers.

Iraq and Iran were still disagreeing about their border. In 1980, Iraq attacked Iran and began a long war. The Iran-Iraq War lasted for eight years. It hurt both countries.

Before Iraq could recover, Hussein ordered an attack on Kuwait in 1990. Iraqis have long believed that Kuwait's land actually

Saddam Hussein

belongs to Iraq. Hussein wanted to conquer Kuwait and sell its oil to help pay for Iraq's war **debts**. Iraq's attack on Kuwait started the Persian Gulf War. A group of countries, including the U.S., banded together to defend Kuwait. The war ended six weeks later with Iraq's defeat.

Today, Iraq is rebuilding after many years of war. But it is difficult. The **UN** established **sanctions** against Iraq. It wants the Iraqi government to allow weapons inspectors into the country. The UN does not want Iraq to have **weapons of mass destruction**.

The sanctions make life hard for Iraqis. They have to **ration** food and medicine. They cannot sell their oil, so they do not have much money to improve their country. Iraq is facing a difficult time in its long history.

An Iraqi mother unpacks her family's food ration.

The Land Between Two Rivers

Iraq is located in southwestern Asia, in the Middle East. Iraq borders Turkey on the north, Syria on the northwest, and Jordan on the west. Iran is Iraq's eastern neighbor. Kuwait and Saudi Arabia are on Iraq's southern border. The Tigris and Euphrates Rivers run through Iraq, where they join together to form the Shatt al-Arab River.

Iraq is divided into two regions. The highland region is home to the northeastern mountains. The lowland region includes the Al-Jazirah **upland**, the **alluvial** plain, and the deserts.

Northeast Iraq has mountains, hills, and plains. It rises from the Al-Jazirah toward the Turkish and Iranian borders. This region has a series of **plateaus**, river basins, and rolling hills. On the border is part of Kurdistan, a mountainous region that extends into Turkey and Iran. The Zagros Mountains have Iraq's only forests. The tallest peak is Mount Halgurd at 12,230 feet (3,728 m).

The Tigris River

The Land Between Two Rivers

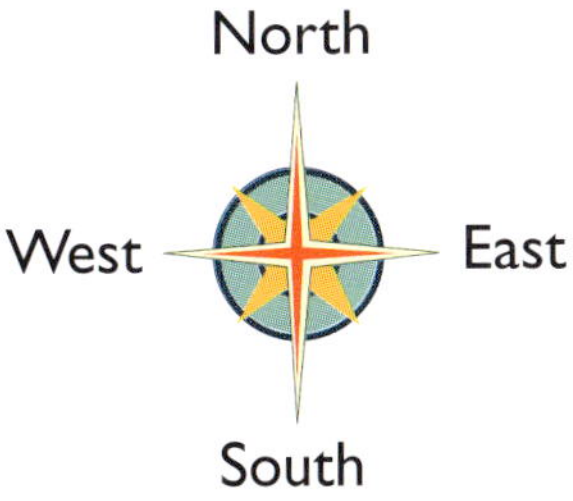

A **plateau** lies between the Tigris and Euphrates Rivers. It is called Al-Jazirah, which means "the island." This **upland** area has several **salt flats**. The largest is Milhat Ashquar.

The **alluvial** plain is shaped like a triangle. It runs from Balad and Ar-Ramadi all the way south to the Persian Gulf. These plains make up almost a third of the country's area. But they are low-lying and often have seasonal flooding.

Deserts cover the western and southern regions of Iraq. The deserts cover almost half of the country. The western desert is called Wadiyah. The southern desert is called Al-Hijarah.

The lowland region has only two seasons, winter and summer. There is hardly any rain during the hot summer. Most of the rain occurs in the cool winter.

In the highland region, there is more rain. It is also colder there. It can even snow in the winter.

Boats carry goods and people along the Shatt al-Arab River.

Rainfall

AVERAGE YEARLY RAINFALL

Inches	Centimeters
Under 10	Under 25
10 - 20	25 - 50
20 - 40	50 - 100

Temperature

Winter

AVERAGE TEMPERATURE

Fahrenheit	Celsius
Over 86°	Over 30°
68° - 86°	20° - 30°
50° - 68°	10° - 20°
32° - 50°	0° - 10°
Under 32°	Under 0°

Summer

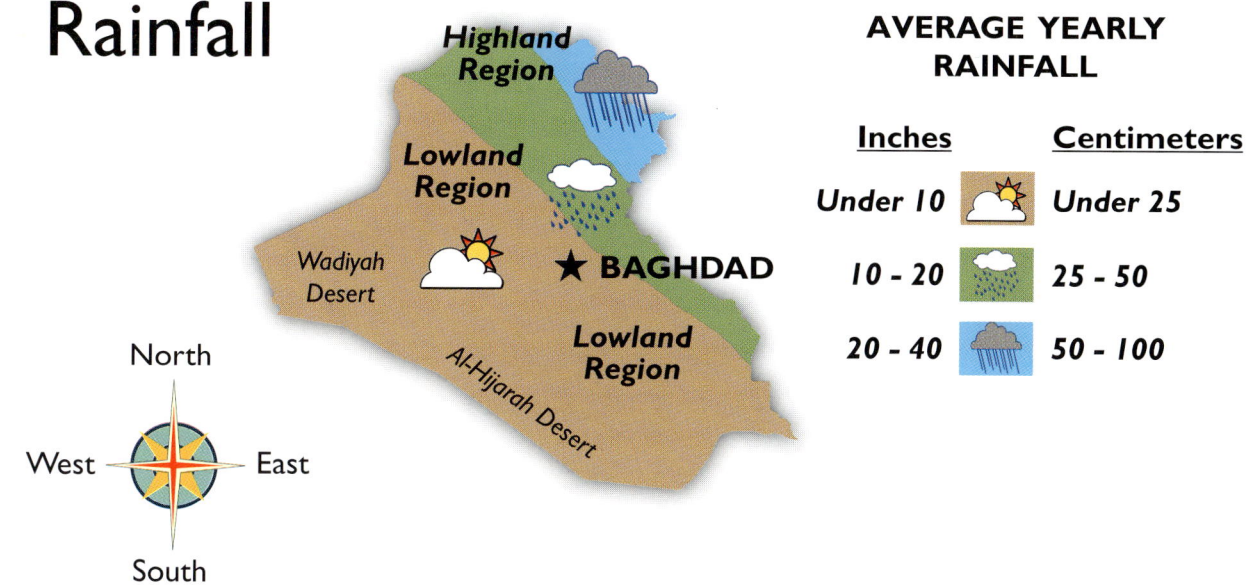

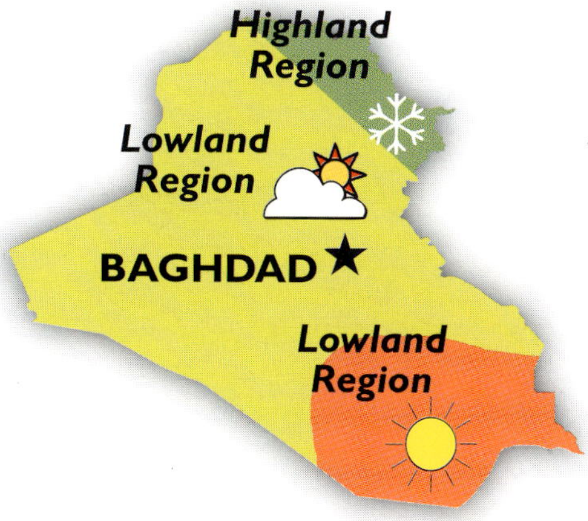

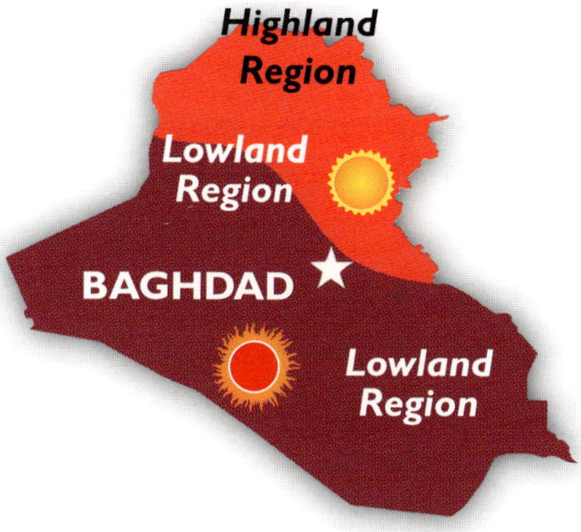

Iraq's Plants & Animals

Iraq's varied land makes it home to many kinds of plants and animals.

Forests are found in the northeast mountains. Hawthorn, junipers, terebinth, and wild pears grow on the lower mountain slopes. Northern Iraqis herd sheep and goats.

Kurdish children in northern Iraq herd their sheep.

A tamarisk tree in desert dunes

In the Al-Jazirah **upland**, mugwort, goosefoot, milkweed, and thyme grow. Farther south toward the deserts, willows, tamarisks, poplars, licorice plants, and bulrushes grow on the banks of the Tigris and Euphrates Rivers. The rivers are full of fish. There are *masgouf*, carp, barbus, catfish, and loach.

In the desert regions, there are not many plants. Tamarisk, milfoil, ziziphus, and salsola grow there. Gazelle can be found in this region. Reptiles also live here. Poisonous vipers and desert black snakes are dangerous.

In the marshlands of the southern **alluvial** plain, there are wild boars. The marbled teal nests in the marshes. Fishermen must watch for hook-nosed and Arabian Gulf sea snakes. Their bite can be fatal.

A marbled teal

Iraq's Government

Iraq is a republic. It has one political party, the Ba'th Party. Iraq's **constitution** provides a system of government made up of three branches called **executive**, **legislative**, and **judicial**.

The president and the RCC hold the executive power. The president is also chairman of the RCC, **premier**, and commander of the armed forces.

Legislative power is given to a group of elected lawmakers. They serve in the National Assembly. Members serve a four-year term.

A system of independent courts called a judiciary holds Iraq's judicial power. Iraq has civil and criminal courts. And it has special courts that deal with things such as national security and agriculture.

At the local level, Iraq is divided into 18 **governorates**. Each governorate has a governor and is divided into smaller areas called districts. There are 91 districts.

Iraq's government works to make Iraq a good country to live in. It is trying to improve education, create opportunities for women, and increase **economic** opportunities for all Iraqis. But the Ba'th Party is very strict. People who disagree with the government can be killed. Iraqis do not have the political freedoms enjoyed in many other countries.

A meeting of the National Assembly

Making Money

Iraq has the second-largest **economy** in the Arab world. Only Saudi Arabia's economy is larger. Oil is Iraq's most important product. It has the world's second-largest oil reserve.

The money Iraq makes from selling its oil has allowed the government to make many improvements. It has completed **irrigation** projects, built roads and railways, and brought electricity to **rural** areas.

Farming is also important to Iraq's economy. Farmers grow fruit, grains, and vegetables. But only a small part of Iraq's land is fit for growing crops. Several dams have been built on the Tigris and Euphrates Rivers. These dams provide water for irrigation.

The river water is silty. The silt makes the crops grow well. But it also blocks the irrigation lines. The water also is salty. The salt builds up in the soil, making it difficult to grow crops. When rivers flood the fields, crops can die.

A worker harvests dates from a date palm tree.

Even with these problems, about a third of Iraq's work force works in agriculture. The main crops are dates, barley, wheat, rice, and vegetables.

Iraq is working to improve its **industries**. **Petrochemical** and iron and steel plants have been built at Khawr az-Zubayr. At Al-Musayyib, oil is **refined** and petrochemicals are produced. Military hardware, tractors, electric goods, and telephone cable are among the goods made in Iraq.

Workers at a Kirkuk petroleum refinery process oil for export.

Most of the goods that Iraqis need are **imported**. The main imports are cars and trucks, industrial and electrical goods, fabrics and clothing, and construction goods. Iraq **exports** oil, dates, cotton, wool, and animal products.

Iraq's Beautiful Cities

Baghdad is Iraq's largest city. About five million people live there. Baghdad was founded in A.D. 762, when Arab rulers chose it as their headquarters. When Iraq gained independence in 1932, Baghdad was chosen as the capital.

The Tigris River divides Baghdad. Its ancient part is on the east bank. There, many old buildings line narrow streets. In the evening, markets come to life.

People worked hard to control flooding on the Tigris River. This allowed a modern part of Baghdad to grow on the river's west bank. There, many new high-rise apartment buildings have been built.

Women shop at the Kadhimiya market in Baghdad. Most Iraqis must buy high-priced food at markets because their government food ration is not enough to feed their families.

Baghdad is the **industrial** center of Iraq. Oil **refineries**, metal works, food processing companies, and other factories are located there. Baghdad is an important trading center. Three railroad lines serve Baghdad. There is also a railroad line to Europe.

Baghdad, Iraq

Baghdad is also Iraq's cultural center. Many of its buildings are from the ancient Mesopotamians. Baghdad has a thirteenth century Abbasid palace. The royal **mausoleum** of King Faisal I is there, too. And Baghdad has three universities and a military academy.

Basra is Iraq's second-largest city. About 700,000 people live there. The Arabs founded it in A.D. 638. Basra is located on the banks of the Shatt al-Arab River. It is 70 miles (110 km) north of the Persian Gulf.

Basra is Iraq's main port. Most of Iraq's products leave the country through Basra. And most of Iraq's oil is processed there. Then, the oil is pumped to the Persian Gulf for **export**. Basra is also an agricultural center. Dates, corn, and rice are grown nearby.

The Iran-Iraq War heavily damaged Basra. The Iranians wanted to stop Iraq from exporting oil and making money. The bombing forced many people to move away. In the years after the war, people have returned to Basra. And the government is working to rebuild its oil **industry**.

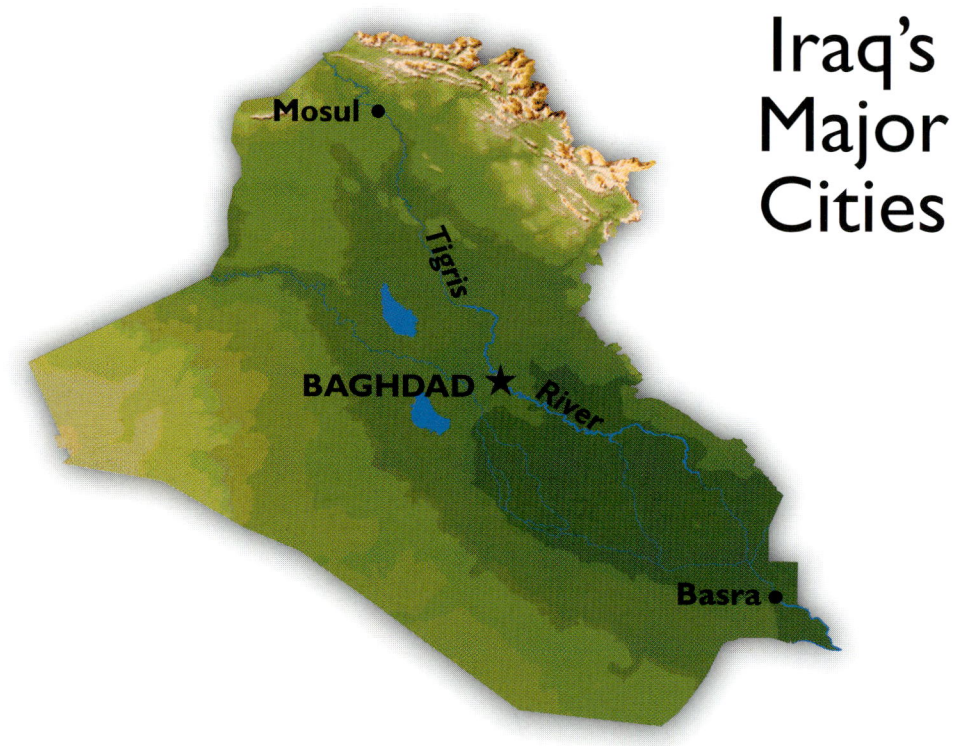

Iraq's Major Cities

Iraq's Beautiful Cities

Iraq's third-largest city is Mosul. Mosul has about 600,000 people. Most of them are Kurds and Christian Arabs. The city is on the west bank of the Tigris River. It is the center of trade for Iraq's northwestern area.

Roads and railroads connect Mosul to Baghdad, Syria, and Turkey. This allows trade with other cities and countries. The people in Mosul make cement, fabrics, sugar, and agricultural products. There are also many large oil fields around Mosul.

Mosul has several important buildings. There's the Great **Mosque**, with its leaning **minaret**. The Red Mosque, the Nabi Jarjis Mosque, and the University of Mosul are there, too.

The leaning minaret on the Great Mosque is 165 feet (50 m) tall and more than 800 years old. Some Iraqis believe it is bowing to the Prophet Mohammed.

Iraq on the Go

Iraq has a vast transportation system. Roads, railroads, waterways, aircraft, and **pipelines** transport Iraq's people and products from place to place.

Almost all of Iraq's roads are paved. Roads connect Iraq with its neighboring countries. The largest road network is in the country's southern part. This area has the greatest population and **industrial** production.

Three main railways serve Iraq. There is a **meter-gauge** line from Baghdad to Kirkuk and Irbil. **Standard-gauge** lines run from Baghdad to Mosul to Turkey. They also run from Baghdad to Basra to Umm Quasir. The government hopes to soon connect all major cities with high-speed rail service.

A memorial to the Iran-Iraq War stretches across a highway in Iraq.

Rivers, lakes, and streams also provide transportation. It is hard to sail on the rivers because of flooding and shallow areas. But steamships can go up the Tigris to Baghdad.

Smaller vessels can go all the way to Mosul. The Euphrates is shallower than the Tigris, and is limited to small crafts. Oceangoing ships can sail inland 85 miles (137 km) to Basra on the Shatt al-Arab.

Iraq's national airline, Iraqi Airways, was founded in 1945. There are international airports at Baghdad and Basra. Iraq also has four regional airports and several military airports.

Oil is transported across Iraq by **pipeline**. Oil pipelines travel over land to seaports for **export**. An important pipeline runs from Kirkuk to the Mediterranean port of Dortyol in Turkey. Another important pipeline travels from Iraq through Kuwait to the Red Sea port of Saudi Arabia. Since Iraq's **economy** depends on exporting oil, pipeline transportation is very important.

To change the direction of the oil flow in this pipeline, an Iraqi oil worker turns the wheel which controls a valve inside the pipe. This pipeline transports oil between Iraq and Turkey. It can carry more than one million gallons (4 million liters) of oil a day.

Citizens of Iraq

Kurdish children

There are many different people in Iraq. The largest groups are the Arabs and the Kurds. There are also Persians, Lurs, Armenians, Turkomans, and Jews.

Arabs are a people united by language, religion, and a shared history. They are not related through bloodlines. Arabs conquered Iraq in the seventh century A.D. Most Iraqis are Arabs. They speak Arabic and are mostly **Muslims**.

The Kurds are the second-largest group in Iraq. They speak Kurdish and are Muslims. They live in three northeastern **governorates** called Kurdistan. There are also Kurds in Iran, Turkey, and Syria.

The Kurds are an ancient people. They have been fighting for an independent nation for many years. But Iraq and its neighboring countries do not want to give land to the Kurds. So, the Kurds and Arabs fight for territory. Iraq's government tries hard to defeat the Kurds. It has even used chemical weapons on them. But the Kurds will not give up.

Though Iraqi people have many differences, they all have families. Iraqi parents usually have five or six children. Iraqi families are made up of a father, mother, sons, sons' wives and children, and unmarried daughters. After a daughter gets married, she lives with her husband's family.

The father is the head of the **traditional** Iraqi family. He makes the family decisions. The mother does most of the household chores. And she cooks the family's meals. She also chooses her sons' wives.

An Iraqi father holds his child. The father is wearing a head covering called a kaffiyeh.

Iraqi families eat dates, spicy kebabs, and *masgouf,* a fish from the Tigris River. Iraqis enjoy *quzi,* a stuffed lamb dish. *Kubba,* a dish of minced meat, nuts, raisins, and spices is also popular. Rice and a flat bread called *samoon* are eaten with most meals.

Iraqi families live in many different kinds of houses. In the country's northern part, many houses are made of stone. In the cities, families live in brick houses and big apartment buildings. In the deserts, tents provide shelter. In the southern marshlands, Iraqis build houses with reeds.

Both boys and girls ages six to twelve must attend a free, primary school for six years. Primary schooling is known as the first level.

The second level of education has two three-year programs. The first three years are known as secondary school. The second three years are called preparatory school.

When students complete their first two levels of education, they can go to a university or technical school. After completing their schooling, Iraqis work at many jobs. They are teachers, government workers, farmers, metal workers, and merchants. Others work in offices and factories.

A school in Saddam City

Date Shakes

There are 25 million date palms growing in Iraq. Dates are Iraq's second-largest **export** item, after oil. Here is a recipe that uses dates.

3/4 cup dates, pitted and chopped
1 1/4 cups milk
1 pint vanilla ice cream

Put the dates and 1/2 cup of the milk in a blender. Blend on high until the mixture is smooth. Add the remaining milk and the ice cream. Blend on low until smooth. Makes 3 – 4 servings.

AN IMPORTANT NOTE TO THE CHEF: Always have an adult help with the preparation and cooking of food. Never use kitchen utensils or appliances without adult permission and supervision.

LANGUAGE

ARABIC

Yes _____	Na'am
No _____	Iaa
Thank You _____	Shokran
Hello _____	Ahalan
Mountain _____	Gabal
Restaurant _____	Matiam
Friend _____	Sadik
Potato _____	Patatis

KURDISH

Cabbage _____	Kelerim
Cake _____	Kek
Day _____	Roj
Cat _____	Pisile
Bakery _____	Nanewaxane
Banana _____	Moz
Almond _____	Badem

Happy Holidays

Iraq enjoys many public holidays. These holidays are like those in many other countries.

In Iraq, January 1 is New Year's Day, just as it is in the United States or Canada. Other public holidays are Labor Day on May 1 and Peace Day on August 8.

Iraq also celebrates many **Islamic** holidays. The dates of the holidays are based on the Islamic or Hijra calendar. Most Iraqis follow this kind of calendar. It has 12 months. But the months are based on the **phases** of the moon. So, a year is 354 and 11/30 days long, instead of 365. As a result, many of Iraq's Islamic holidays have different dates each year.

Iraqis celebrate Eid al-Fitr at an amusement park in Baghdad.

One of these holidays is Mawild an Nabi. This is the birthday of the Prophet Mohammed. He is the founder of **Islam**.

During the Islamic month of Ramadan, **Muslims** are not allowed to eat or drink from dawn until dusk. When the month is over, people celebrate. They have a large festival called Eid al-Fitr, or the Feast of Fastbreaking.

A family eats together after sundown during Ramadan.

Relaxing in Iraq

In Iraq, people enjoy many kinds of sports. Iraqis like to swim, play basketball, and watch boxing. The national sport of soccer is also the most popular.

Iraq has many soccer teams. Many games are played in Al-Shaab Stadium in Baghdad. Ahmed Radhi is Iraq's most popular soccer player. He scored Iraq's only World Cup goal in 1986.

Iraq has many museums for people to enjoy. The National Museum and the Museum of Arab Antiquities are in Baghdad. People also visit the Baghdad Institute of Fine Arts and the National Museum of Modern Art.

Iraqi boys play soccer in a Baghdad park.

Iraqis also enjoy many kinds of music. The National Symphony Orchestra performs in Baghdad. But most Iraqis enjoy **traditional** folk music. Folk music is played on the *oud*, a type of lute, the *rebab*, a type of fiddle, and the *kanoon*, a type of harp.

Poetry is another popular pastime in Iraq. Iraqi poets such as Muhammad Mahdi al-Jawahiri and Nazik al-Malaika are well known throughout the Arab world.

Leisure activities allow Iraqis an opportunity to have a good time. This is important in a land where every day is hard because of **economic sanctions**.

Iraqi people struggle to get food, clothing, and shelter. The government works to keep the country operating without the money from selling oil.

But the **UN** wants to stop Iraq's **aggressive** government from invading other countries and hurting people. It believes that the sanctions are the best way to do this.

When the UN and Iraq's government can reach an agreement, the sanctions will end, and Iraq will be able to **import** and **export** products again. And one of the world's great nations will continue to contribute to world history.

Glossary

aggressive - displaying hostile actions.
alliance - people, groups, or nations united for a common cause.
allies - a group united in an alliance.
alluvial - made up of sediment left by flowing water.
constitution - the main principles that govern a city, state, or country.
constitutional monarchy - a form of government with a king or queen. He or she must follow the laws of the constitution.
contribution - the act of giving something to others.
coup - a sudden overthrow of an established government.
debt - money that is owed.
economy - the way a country uses it money, goods, and natural resources.
executive - the branch of a government that puts laws into effect.
export - to send goods to another county to sell or trade.
governorate - a political district within a country.
import - to bring in goods from another country to sell or trade.
industry - all of a country's manufacturing plants, businesses, and trade.
irrigation - using channels, streams, or pipes to supply land with water.
Islam - the religious faith of Muslims. It is based on the teachings of Mohammed as they appear in the Koran.
judicial - the branch of a government that administers the laws.
legislative - the branch of a government that makes laws.
mausoleum - a large tomb, usually built of stone.
meter gauge - a railroad that has 3.3 feet (1 m) between its tracks.
minaret - a tall tower on a mosque. Minarets have balconies from which Muslims are called to prayer.
mosque - a Muslim place of worship.
Muslim - a person who follows Islam.
Palestine - a region in southwestern Asia on the Mediterranean Sea.
petrochemical - a chemical that comes from petroleum or natural gas.
phase - the shape of the lighted part of the moon at a given time.
pipeline - pipes that carry gas and oil.
plateau - a raised piece of land with a level surface.
premier - the highest-ranked member of a government, also called a prime minister.
ration - a fixed amount of food that has to last an exact amount of time.
rebellion - an armed attack on a government.

refine - to make something pure.
rural - out in the country, not in the city.
salt flat - a large, flat piece of land that has salty soil.
sanction - a measure by several nations against another nation that has violated international law. Sanctions are meant to force the offending nation to comply with the law.
socialism - a kind of economy. The government or the citizens control the production and distribution of goods.
standard gauge - a railroad that has 4.7 feet (1.4 m) between its tracks.
traditional - knowledge and beliefs handed down from one generation to another.
United Nations (UN) - an organization of nations formed in 1945 to promote peace, security, and economic development.
upland - the higher part of a piece of land.
weapons of mass destruction - weapons that have the power to kill many people at one time.

Web Sites

Iraq: A Country Study
http://lcweb2.loc.gov/frd/cs/iqtoc.html
The Library of Congress sponsors this site on Iraq. It has extensive information on Iraq's history, society, economy, government and politics, and military.

CIA: The World Factbook 1999 - Iraq
http://www.odci.gov/cia/publications/factbook/iz.html
This site by the CIA offers up-to-date statistics on Iraq. It has sections on Iraq's geography, people, government, economy, communications, transportation, and military.

These sites are subject to change. Go to your favorite search engine and type in "Iraq" for more sites.

Index

A
Abbasids 9, 25
al-Bakr, Ahmad Hassan 11, 12
Al-Hijarah 16
al-Ilah, Abd 10
al-Jawahiri, Muhammad Mahdi 37
Al-Jazirah plateau 16
Al-Jazirah upland 14, 18
al-Malaika, Nazik 37
Al-Musayyib 23
al-Nayif, Abd ar-Razzaq 11
Al-Shaab Stadium 36
Alexander the Great 9
alluvial plain 14, 16, 19
animals 4, 18, 19
Ar-Ramadi 16
Arab League 10
Arab-Israeli War 10
Arabs 4, 8, 10, 24, 25, 27, 30
Armenians 30
Asia 14
Assyrians 9

B
Babylon 8, 9
Babylonians 8
Baghdad 4, 9, 24, 25, 27, 28, 29, 36, 37
Balad 16
Basra 25, 26, 28, 29
Ba'th Party 11, 20, 21

C
climate 16
Code of Hammurabi 8
cuneiform 8
Cyrus the Great 9

D
deserts 4, 14, 16, 18, 19
Dortyol 29

E
economy 4, 22, 25, 26, 27
Eid al-Fitr 35
Euphrates River 4, 14, 16, 19, 22, 29

F
Faisal I, King 9, 10, 25
Faisal II, King 10
families 31
farming 4, 8, 11, 22, 23, 26

food 13, 31, 35, 37
forests 14, 18

G
Ghazi, King 10
government 5, 9, 10, 11, 20, 21, 26, 30, 37
Great Mosque 27

H
Hammurabi, King 8, 9
holidays 34, 35
houses 32
Hussein, Saddam 11, 12, 13

I
Iran 12, 14, 30
Iran-Iraq War 12, 26
Irbil 28
Islam 4, 9, 11, 30, 34, 35

J
Jews 30
Jordan 14

K
Kassem, Karim 10
Khawr az-Zubayr 23
Kirkuk 28, 29
Kurdistan 14, 30
Kurds 4, 12, 27, 30, 31
Kuwait 12, 13, 14, 29

L
Lurs 30

M
Mawild an Nabi 35
Mediterranean Sea 29
Mesopotamia 8, 9, 25
Middle East 4, 14
Milhat Ashquar salt flats 16
Mongols 9
Mosul 27, 28, 29
Mount Halgurd 14
mountains 4
museums 36
music 37

N
Nabi Jarjis Mosque 27
National Assembly 20

National Symphony Orchestra 37
Nebuchadnezzar, King 9

O
oil 4, 5, 11, 13, 22, 23, 25, 26, 29, 37

P
Palestine 10
Persian Gulf 16, 25, 26
Persian Gulf War 13
Persians 30
plains 4
plants 4, 18, 19
Prophet Mohammed 35

R
Radhi, Ahmed 36
railways 22, 25, 27, 28
Ramadan 35
Red Mosque 27
Red Sea 29
Revolutionary Command Council 11, 20
roads 22, 27, 28

S
sanctions 5, 13, 37
Saudi Arabia 14, 22, 29
school 32
Shatt al-Arab River 14, 25, 29
sports 4, 36
Sumerians 8
Syria 14, 27, 30

T
Tigris River 4, 14, 16, 19, 22, 24, 27, 28, 29, 31
Turkey 14, 27, 28, 29, 30
Turkomans 30
Turks 8, 9

U
Umm Quasir 28
United Nations 10, 13, 37
universities 25, 27

W
Wadiyah 16
World War I 9
World War II 10

Z
Zagros Mountains 14